# Just Once

To Phyllis —

with love + fondest
memories.

PEACE.
Jamie Pinley

Also by the same author

*Paper Doves, Falling and Other Poems*

*The Loneliness of Blizzards*

*Cloud: A Poem in 2 Acts*

*The Wounded Table: Prose Poems*

*no stars, no moon: new and collected haiku*

*Ikon: Poems*

# Just Once

Poems by

Jamie Parsley

Loonfeather Press
Bemidji, Minnesota

Cover Design: Mary Lou Marchand
Cover Art: *November Moon* by Geri Burkhart Weiner

First printing 2007
Printed in Canada
ISBN 0926147-24-2

This project is made possible, in part, by a grant from the Region
2 Arts Council through funding by the Minnesota State Legisla-
ture.

Thanks too to the North Dakota Council on the Arts, which re-
ceived funding from the North Dakota State Legislature and the
National Endowment for the Arts for a grant which enabled these
poems to be completed.

Loonfeather Press
P.O. Box 1212
Bemidji, MN 56619

**for Joyce Parsley**

*—after a poem by Marina Tsvetaeva*

Grant her health,
and to her quiet bedside
send the Angel
which flew so silently from me.
Keep her as she is—
shunning too much talk,
and let her not fall,
like me, in love a little with death.

"You see
the cut and hear the scream
but don't perceive or understand
and aren't supposed to,
lest you be forgiven."

—Tim Dlugos

# Foreword

These poems were written over the course of my 32nd year—from December to December. It was a year of one set-back after another, the major one being my diagnosis with cancer on February 20. In the months that followed, I went through a rigorous course of radiation, including the side effects of the treatment. And, ultimately, by the end of the year, I had, for the most part, recovered. It was a year of few highs and several devastating lows. It was one of the most memorable—and most difficult—years of my life.

I responded to these setbacks the only way I—as a poet—knew how to respond to them: I funneled and processed the experiences into these poems. The poems themselves emerged from the daily experiences of my cancer much as they appear before you now. Although each was revised—sometimes several times—they maintain their basic initial structure and form. Despite decreased physical energy, somehow I found a reserve of internal energy that allowed these poems to be made—sometimes two or three in a single day. On the day I was diagnosed—February 20—I wrote four poems alone.

No one was more amazed than I by the rate with which these poems came. I was reminded quite often as I wrote them, of a reference the British critic A. Alvarez made regarding Sylvia Plath's sudden (and sadly, last) creative spurt: he said it seemed as though, when the devil takes a poet by the throat—when the hard things of life happen—the poet needs to be ready for them. Certainly, this diagnosis was one of those moments in my life in which "the devil"—that personification of every fear and darkness—had in fact taken me by the throat and shaken me. And I was ready for it in ways that surprised and startled me.

I wrote them in a single notebook— which ironically featured a bevy of skeletons engaging in a kind of danse macabre on its cover—in waiting rooms, in cars, in hospital cafeterias, in doctor's offices and in changing rooms between X-rays.

As each successive year leads me further away from that unique and frightening year, I view these collective poems as a sort of poignant *memento mori*. They remind me of not only my own brush with something potentially lethal and of my own mortality, they are also, to quote George Herbert, "all a case of knives." They were, in the truest sense, the instruments I used to scythe and pare the sometimes overwhelming and disconcerting experiences of confronting and overcoming my own cancer.

Somehow, I emerged from that year changed. I came away stronger and more sure of myself. I came away transformed in ways I can not now even begin to fully explain or articulate. Hopefully these poems are able to give voice in some way to that transformation and rejuvenation.

*—Jamie Parsley*
*January 2006*
*Fargo, North Dakota*

# Acknowledgments

Grateful acknowledgment is made to the editors and publishers of the following publications in which the following poems first appeared, some in a slightly different form:

"Otro" in *Albatross;* "Pelvis" in *Angel Face;* "Let's Wait" in *Ascent;* "Almost Pentecost" in *Avenues;* "Thursday in the Fourth Week of Lent" and "St. David's Day" in *The Blackwood Press DUB;* "I Float" in *The Curbside Review;* "To the Floor" and "Ophanim" in *Ellipses;* "Easter" in *Horizon Lines;* "Echo" in *Red Corral;* "Mask," "Desk 42," "Sh'ma" and "Resuscitation" in *The Sheaf;* "Eye" in *Sunspinner;* "Bed Sheet" and "Horizon" in *Tamafyhr Mountain Poetry;* "Skein " in *Thunder Sandwich;* "Just Once" in *White Crane Journal.*

"Ophanim" and "Horizon" originally appeared in the anthology, *Becoming Fire: Spiritual Writing from Rising Generations,* The Andover Newton Theological School, Newton Centre, MA, 2005.

Very special thanks to my father, Al Parsley, for his continued love and support, to Betty Rossi for her patient editing of these poems, to Mary Lou Marchand for her invaluable comments and to Gail Rixen for her long friendship and her patient and much-appreciated criticisms. Also my deepest appreciation to The Reverend Ann Anderson, Greg Bachmeier, Andrea Berninger, the late Sister Imogene Blatz, OSB, Sharon Chmielarz, The Right Reverend Andrew Fairfield, Leslie and Jonathan Flom, Christie Grandbois, The Reverend Deacon Mary Gokey, Mike and Linda Liebert-Hall, the late Dr. Jim Jacobson, Brother Benet Tvedten, OSB, Carla Smith, The Right Reverend Michael Smith, The Reverend Mark Strobel, The Right Reverend John Thornton, Barbara Williams, Larry Woiwode, Leisha Woltjer and to the parishioners of Gethsemane Episcopal Cathedral in Fargo.

Special thanks, of course, to the staff at the Roger Maris Cancer Center in Fargo and the doctors and nurses who treated me at MeritCare Hospital in Fargo.

# Contents

## V. "I lay myself in these wounds . . ."

## VI. *O benediction!*

# I

# The Future Rises

"*...from strength to strength...*"
—The Book of Common Prayer

# Let's Wait

*after a poem by Pablo Neruda*

The future rises like
bread. We wait for it
the same way we wait for

medicine at the pharmacy
or a package in the mail.
The days seem to be made

in a factory somewhere
where workers of the soul
build them and weigh

them and prepare them—
days that, terrible or
beautiful, will knock at

your door in their own time
to either give you an orange,
dripping with juice, or to

strike you on the face with
a wind so cold you will stand there gasping
for your next breath.

*December*

# Just Once

*a fragment after Rilke*

Being in this place—
in this heady instant—
means everything.


Everything needs us. This
temporary moment—
which for some reason

neither you nor I will ever
completely understand—
keeps whispering our names—

you and I who stand
here, transparent as shadows.
Just once—not one thing

more. And you and I also—just
once. Once is enough.
You and I to have been one

with the earth—
with everything beneath us,
this sacred ground

on which we tread without
a thought or a prayer—
can never be taken from us.


*January 25*

# Skein

In the latest dream—
which came upon me angry

as a flash flood—something happened
to my body—something so secret I didn't quite

know what it was. Some
force against force pulverized

my flesh into a skein of unidentifiable
fragments—bits of bones,

broken skin and veins,
a sorry dark residue left

on the sheets behind
me like an imprint. All of this

awaited the grave swathed
in a linen bag, encased by epoxy

in a chest of polished *rosso laguna* marble
as I—oblivious to the destruction done to me—

listened for a voice—a distant
whisper of my name to which

I could respond with either
shy apprehension or a joy so full

I would leap up from that place and race
through clouds and high-flying contrails.

*January 27*

# To the Floor

*—for Andrea Berninger*

By this time of the night the moon
has fallen from its place on
the wall. Do we know
where it will go? To the

floor? To the bookshelf? Or
to the mirror where it
will reflect itself
reflecting the sun?

The moon is falling
and I am watching it,
waiting for it to sigh
or breathe or hiss as though

it were full of white steam. Stars
no longer interest me. Clouds
pale in comparison.
I think I may have

part of the moon within me—
something pale and cold
and chalky as plaster.
But round—

a perfect, unbroken circle
even despite the pocked
shadows and the luminous
edges of bone.

*February 12*

# There

The winter sparrows all at once
are quiet. I heard them and now
I don't. Something thuds instead in
my head like a disjointed dream—
a queasy realization that whirs and turns

within me like well-oiled hinges.
My head pulses but not *it*—it!—
huddled there. No, it doesn't pulse
or thud. I think it's dead—
dead like a stone is dead. Only it's

there. *There!* Snow hisses at
the window and I feel like I'm
going to fall against a wall.
But I can't. I can't
cup it even. It's that big,

that far swollen beyond
my flat pink palm, beyond the
last reaching fingertip. The
winter sparrows are hushed
into a silence deeper than

this unending winter. They have fled
into a sky grayer than their gray
shadows. They have left a hushed
silence in the place they just fled,
there, just beneath my bedroom window

where pale light falls. It falls
there and makes the gray snow yellow,
where all the twig-like tracks of the birds
are laid out like the words of this poem.
There. Just there.

*February 15*

# HealthLine

*It blooms!* I sing into the phone's mouthpiece.
It's there, in the limp I try so hard to hide. It

swells into a solid growth I can no longer
cover with two or three layers of clothes.

The nurse, off in that distant sweet place
on the other end of the line, says my name

with such a familiar ease I wonder if she knows
me, if she has always known about this

secret I reveal to her and only her.
Is there pain? she asks. *No.* How large is it?

How long have you had it? A long pause after my answer
and then, *How* long?

The floor goes then, taking
me with it. I am gone,

floating off to a distant place not that
different from the one that exists

at the end of the phone line. In that place,
her voice is commanding. She says,

"Tomorrow." *Tomorrow,* I repeat.
Then, she's gone—

her voice swallowed up now
by the lulling signal. In it, I hear

*Tomorrow*—that simple hum.
*Tomorrow,* like some vague voice of hope.

*February 15*

# I Float

What could it be that sings
at my arm's hub? What is it
that doesn't leave even

half-moon shadows on
the skin? It clicks.
*That* I know. Something

clatters in its climb from
the wrist to the forearm to
the shoulder and then down.

Down—
a chain-reaction of some sort,
there under my skin.

Bloated veins, like an addict's,
come showing through—
blue and thin. Even then, it can't

be seen or smelled or grasped.
Doused in an exhaust of blood,
the wrists sigh with a steady, cadenced

pulse. The cuticles glow, pale and distant,
at the ends of my fingers like
moons. And that's all. No dull

throbbing in the neck. No
ache persistent as a virus.
What pain there is

is unremarkable. I float,
fanning down toward some
hidden delta. I float,

lulled into complacency
by a pulse so gentle it's almost
like prayer at Compline.

*February 16*

# Mask

I know what I wish it was—a
hernia, displacing itself, or
fluid (*what's the word?*

*a hydrocele?*) dammed to a reservoir.
Not this—this thing whose name
I certainly will not say. I will not use that

dangerous word that dirties my tongue
and ruins my day right to hell—
this day that should be like any other

spring day. Look how the snow melts. I should
be glad about the thaw. No, I shouldn't be sitting
here shocked into a silence that leaves me weak and

teary. I should be laughing about how
ridiculous it was to get so upset over
a growth—a simple

nameless lump, harmless as a bee
sting. But it isn't harmless. It has a name—
a name my poor physician simply refused

to repeat when he saw it
just this morning and gasped,
"Oh God!" *Oh God,* my head
sang as I watched

him reach across his desk to call
the urologist. *Oh God, Oh God,*
the dull thud in my throat repeated

11

as I walked from the office and sat
down in my car. *Oh God,* I intoned
to the windshield streaked with the

last watery traces of this morning's snow.
So, the mask's off. I've left on the floor
my last ounce of hope. In the rearview mirror

I can see it there on my face—that
cold look—gray as a stone. It's
set into place—my complacent

expression sweet as sin. I'm opaque.
See how I bite my lip. See how I jut my jaw
so no one can see how undone I am.

How I wish it was not this at all but
my appendix grumbling like low thunder
on the other hip. But no. Not today. Today, let's just

smile—smile, reflection!—and let's
just wish each other well, or at least
as well as can be expected.


*February 18*

# Feeler

Overwhelmed! I have been
completely done in. I am

sullen on this afternoon
that smells ominously like

cedar. Hope is going. It is being
washed away with the laundry. It

churns there. The steel cylinder
tosses it away with the shirt

I wore to the doctor, and the worn
socks wet with snow. The detergents

shift and liquefy into something
hygienic. The yellow powders

mix and make sunlight—
sunlight! in the water. O!

let's face it! Let's be
honest with this . . .

*this,* whatever it is. We'll
beat this too, you know.

Of course we will. Despite
the emotions we wear on

our sleeves for all
the world to see

we're stoic. We're good AngloCatholic
Episcopalians, after all. It's

just another trip-up, another
jarring lurch on that ride to

some distant place
we can only vaguely

envision and we
never, never have

the decency
to discuss.


*February 18*

# II

# February 20

*"The force of the storm does not surprise you"*
—Rilke

## Sh'ma

What is it you hear, Doctor,
in your cold dumb stethoscope?
What is it you feel in that perfectly
professional caress of yours? In that
one movement, that one grasping clutch,
all is made so clear. Try to describe it for me.
Dumb it right down, using the language
I would know. Think poetic legalese.

A *humming* you say? Yes. It's humming
coming up from someplace deep inside me.

The pulse moves. My blood is
wild at the wrist. My heartbeat,
my precious purple drum
rolls and roils
and churns within my chest.
It burns with a fire
so intense not even
your weak medicines
can put it out. Not even that ornery
appendix which roars to life two or
three times a year like some forgotten
angry fetus, can be comparable.

It's something so much worse—so
malevolent in fact that it's completely
sure of itself. It has intent and
its intentions are bad. And still,
it sings! It's singing, doctor!
It sings its intentions to you like
some lulling biological melody.
And the amazing thing is
it doesn't hurt even a little.

So, what caused this? Was it the beef
I ate, the cigarettes I snuck in high school?
Did my body mature too early? Or too late?
What spell was sung against my flesh
at some early age for some
misdeed I no longer remember?

If I didn't do this, then who did?

Let me hear it, Doctor! Let me
listen to the psalm—
that shout of dark lament. I know hymns
better than you know medicine. I'll know
the tune, the meter. I'll wow you with
my knowledge of composers.

Listen to those voices! They're
the eunuchs Shadrach, Meshach
and Abednego. The king of Babylon
has locked them up in a secret place
within me. He's toasting them
like Jersey dogs in the retort of
this fevered churning within me
while his own armored men
scald at the ear.

They're muttering. They're chanting
my boiling blood like a mantra.
They're singing something guttural
and exotic. I can hear them even—

> *Sh'ma yisroayl*
> *Adonoy Elohaynu*
> *Adonoy echod*

Listen! Their prayers bellow
as the heat rises
in a fanning brilliance.

Listen! They are singing! singing
as only a steam whistle can to
the nameless, uninvoked God
who, in my innermost thoughts,
dwells.

*February 20*

# Benign

*1. In the next room*

Listen to them giggle! Listen to that
sweet young couple—blond as a noonday sun—
in the next room. Listen to them coo
every time the nurse goes on—
and God! does the woman go on—
explaining the strange cuneiform images
on the ultrasound's screen. "There's the head," she sings.
"And there's one hand—see the fingers—
and the other—clenching and unclenching like
a second heart there. And look at that spine—
the constellations don't even look *that* beautiful
do they? So," she asks, "do you know the sex?"
And they squeal and clap their hands and sing,
"Of course, it's a boy!" "It's a boy," the nurse repeats
and chuckles to herself as though she knew all along.

It's a boy! and so am I. Even my nurse
is a boy. But he doesn't giggle. He doesn't
go on and on about what he sees in my ultrasound
like some joyful bird. He doesn't
say a thing, his stubbled jaw set like
the emotionless wooden mask from Kenya
on the wall of my study.

He doesn't sing at all. But then, why
should he? What is there to sing about
in this dark cold room. He's only doing
his unpleasant job, gazing first
at the healthy one. It glides there
on the screen, big as the moon. It slides
through the thick lips of skin
white and oval as an egg. It's healthy!

It's so beautifully normal!
Then without a word he slides
the paddle over the other one
and the screen darkens. His jaw
becomes more firm, his eyes turn
gray. I look away at the dark wall
as the couple in the next room
guffaw over the miracle. It's a miracle!
don't you know?


*2. Afterward*

I wait. Here in this perfectly square
changing booth I wait for another nurse—
how many nurses does that make today?—
to fetch me for a chest X-ray.

In the next booth, a doctor sings a new
song to the woman who sat there nervously
humming to herself when I
came back. "Good news!" this song goes.
"It's benign." And she sighs that wonderful,
purifying sigh I long to sigh this afternoon as I
shiver in this cold room, hugging
my shirt and pants to my
lap. "It's benign," she repeats and,
hearing herself, she repeats it
again. "Benign." And even though I
can't see her, I know she's
smiling. She's smiling and, for some
reason I can't even begin to explain, I'm
smiling for her.

I'm smiling when the nurse
knocks at the door and calls
my name, which sounds nothing like
the word "benign," no matter how
I try to pronounce it. *Benign.*

*Benign.* I whisper it before I open
the door and step out, its
very slight echo falling flat and utterly
pointless to the floor of the cubicle
I just left.

My throat is dry—I'm suddenly
so thirsty—and if I said anything at all
I know it would come out of my mouth
cracked and lifeless. Still, I repeat
it like some desperate
incantation—*benign. Benign,* as though I
could change the terrible course this
day has taken—this winding dark
way that will lead me . . . *where?*


3. *To the X-ray*

The nurse leads me through
the winding hallways toward
the X-ray. As she does, the woman
from the next booth passes us. On her face
a faint pink smile kneads
swirled dimples into her fat cheeks. She
doesn't know me, who sat listening in
on her exultant news like some breathless
voyeur. She smiles only to herself as she
passes me and makes her way out of this place.

And then, finally, *they* bound past—
the young couple, arm in
arm, blond as daisies. Twittering like
the sun they both paw at her swollen
gut which contains their every hope

21

and dream. Beaming in this brilliant
moment, they don't even notice the smile
I force at them. But how could they? How
could they—in this glorious moment—
even comprehend the shadow I carry within me
that made my boy nurse look so glum?

They simply pass by and disappear around
the far corner as the nurse leads me—
weak-kneed and dazed—toward the X-ray room
which lies ahead of me, cold as a photographer's studio.


*February 20*

# III

# Three February Poems

*after three Georgia O'Keeffe paintings*

*"Now the sun is bright over what looks a vast field of snow, stretching all the way to the horizon. . . . It is odd to look out on this field of snow or white cotton—It looks almost solid enough to walk on."*

—Georgia O'Keeffe

# Black Rock

*the ultrasound*

This isn't art.
Certainly it's no O'Keeffe—
her *Black Rock with*

*Blue III* or even
her *Black Rock*
*with Red?* Surely I—

a poet, not a painter—
could never have
produced a murky

mass quite *this*
murky within me!
Even if I could would I

have folded in
this uneven balance
of jet black and two-tone

gray? My unsure fingers
longed to produce
this sandy texture yet can't.

Still, there it is in its
macabre light, swimming
jerky and oblivious.

It floats—
so sure of itself—
so steady and confident

as it grows. It
grows! It breathes! It . . . lives!
It lives and moves.

Should I name it?
Should I flaunt it like
my young-faced friends

do with their badly drawn
fetuses, which peer out
doughy and pig-headed

from the chalkboards of
*their* ultrasounds? Should I
caw over it and trace its rounded

outlines like they do? What should
I do other than lie
here, smeared in cold jelly,

letting my body produce
this counterfeit art on
the blue screen above my head?


*February 20*


25

# Pelvis

What is it you
see there? Is there

sky, like O'Keeffe's
*Pelvis* series—dark blue

at the circle swirling
to a light blue at

the vortex? Or is it
something darker and

more vicious? Is it that
nameless gnawing we

know and avoid so well?
How I wish—I wish!

I wish!—it was sky! The
blue sky is so far away today,

hidden from me at this
moment by one concrete

hospital floor after another
and even beyond it,

by layers and layers of
cold gray clouds.

Oh, blue! blue
like the sky over Abiquiu,

where O'Keeffe, holding up
a bleached pelvis bone that

once gave life and was now
lifeless—saw life—

gorgeous blue life
staring back at her

through the emptiness
with its single unblinking eye.

*February 20*

# Clouds

Tile after white tile
glides on the ceiling
above me like Georgia
O'Keeffe's *Sky Above Clouds*

series—the ones she observed,
half-blind, from the oval
window of a sleek
1960s airliner. I am

gazing up at them
from below—
squared white
lights and tiles alternating

as I float toward some
unseen yellow destination
feet-first where something
secret and terrible

will happen to me.
Some deep dark part of me—
some hard black mass—
will be wrestled free

and laid dangerous
and lethal at my hip.
I am flying! blurry-eyed
and dizzy I am going!

And there is nothing
in all the world to stop me now.
I am going! swathed in
clouds and white light

just like Georgia O'Keeffe.
I am going! I am going! etherized
by a misplaced iv whose
blood-filled cord trails me, flailing.


*February 21*

# IV

# By the River Chebar

*"I loved what the doctors took:
the firing calliope of his life.
And clawed the sky like him
pursuing some lovely dimension."*

—James L. White

# *Forråde*

If only I were more Norwegian
my still-numb tongue could
pronounce the word more perfectly.
*Betrayal.* It lies on my tongue

like stitches. It was the very first word
in my dry mouth when I awoke
this morning. The taste of it
made me heave. Before leaving

for the hospital, I went into my workroom
and there it was, in everything
I touched as though for the last time.
The pencil, with my misspelled

name in gilt. The reflection of my face—
purse-lipped and heavily shadowed
like Veronica's veil—in the monitor's
reflection. The imprint

my body made in the deep blue
cushions of the chair.
*Forråde.*
Not my numbed fingers or

my crooked white toes. Not the right
knee sighing with aches, not
the back—disjointed by the collision
of cars—cracking and hissing,

the pain dulled by four years.
No, the betrayal comes from
a place more intimate—more vital
and secret. It tears its way through

my life, through this day that's going—
it's going so quickly I don't know
how to react. It's going! off to a place
dark and cold. Oh, this morning

is the worst—it hurts even to
live it. Nothing is the way it
should be. The sunlight is slightly
dusty. The snow on the sill sags

and turns gray. Even the cold
hangs near the ceiling like
a stain. The morning too has
turned against me like this

body. And I can't find a word in all the world
to make it better. If only I were more
Norwegian—more blond, more sky-
eyed. If only my tongue could trill. Oh God! If only . . .

*February 21*

# Ophanim

I struggle slowly
through foggy layers of

carefully administered
anesthesia. Light floods

to its whorl. Within it,
the ends came together

and at its knot I gasp. What I exhale
is empty air—

grim as Bach—
which floats above me

pale and ghostly. This is
what I've become

in only a matter of minutes. Yesterday
there was none of this, no

fevered visions, no
cyclonic sensations.

Yesterday was . . .
*yesterday.* Now, the firmament

has become the color of terrible
crystal. And I have become circular

and full of movement—
going this way and that

at once. I have become
angelic—

see, I am *glowing*
in this etherized state

yet not like the putti-cherubs
from the Tempio Malatestiano

in Rimini or
the Hungarian ikons of

thin-lipped seraphs. Rather I have
become a flaming wheel

from Ezekiel's gleaming
vision by the river Chebar—

caressing wings
and blinking eyes

circling toward a swirling
nexus of light—

circling, circling! blazing wheels
within blazing wheels.

Circling and swirling
toward an amber-colored

shadow, infested with
stars. See how it struggles at

the knuckle of some massive
left hand. The fingers unfold and . . .

the eyes flutter. The empyrean
dulls and a light so much more

inglorious flows slowly,
ebbing and sighing, into

such an uncertain and
uncomfortable consciousness.


*February 21*

# Resuscitation

*—for Ann Anderson*

I awake! not a resurrection
so much as a resuscitation
like Lazurus, only so much

less dramatic. No forceful
Aramaic voice calls me forth.
There is no one waiting

at the door of this vault
from which I peer
blurry-eyed and dumb.

I am swathed—
white cloth on white
skin. A numbness glides

through my motionless
limbs like a caress as I lie
forgotten in a dark corner,

a gnawing at my side
growing bolder.
The recovery room nurse

finally appears, bitter-faced and frowning.
In between absences she leans near
to my numb face and breathes

on me the sourest of smells.
No, this is not Resurrection, my reeling
thoughts confirm. *I ache!* I whisper, but she

hushes me and disappears—
gone someplace beyond my
blurred frame of vision.

Before I went under—
the student nurse jabbing
and missing the vein twice

with the iv—
I recited to myself—
as though it were

the strongest of incantations—
a stanza from a poem
by Tim Dlugos—

> *I hope that death will lift me*
> *by the hair like an angel*
> *in a Hebrew myth, snatch me with*
> *the strength of sleep's embrace,*
> *and gently set me down*
> *where I'm supposed to be*
> *in just the right place.*

Now lying here, I remember
it and recite it again to myself,
hoping it will release me—hoping

in a hope that seems more distant
by the moment. And as I hope
Tim Dlugos, black-haired and pale as an Italian

saint with his horn-rimmed glasses, is off
in some sweet, pink-hued heaven,
a Postulant for Holy Orders, like me,

for all eternity. The nurse finally
reappears, growls at me when
I groan quietly and rolls me

into the hallway. I am the last
to leave this strange tomb. I float
before her, embalmed and shrouded,

emerging from a clutching
dankness into a whiteness
so bright, I almost can't imagine

anything could be so
beautiful. It lies there
trembling just beyond my

reach, edged in pink. All I can
think as I am rolled
toward the crowded

hallway is that,
maybe this *is*
Resurrection after all.

Maybe—
just maybe—
this *is* Easter morning.


*February 23*

# Angel

The angel's face
carved on the headboard
whispers like the hush
of medication
in my blood.

His cheeks
pucker. What he exhales
onto my cold face smells of
walnut and varnish.
He leans close

and the room fills with
singing! a singing only I—
in this heady moment, still
lethal myself after having
been touched by

something so lethal—
can hear. I gasp! It *is*
the sound of singing!
*singing!* perfect German Baroque
more Protestant than I can

ever hope to be. On the headboard
the angel head frowns. His face sinks at
the grained crease. Gray—
grayer still, the bed sheets
deepen with shadows.

All day—through a steady
counted-out cache of pills and
tepid water—everything
I can even imagine or hope for
stinks either of ink or rotting stars.

*February 25*

# O! the Fingers!

This is where
the scalpel went in—
peeling me in two

revealing the hissing dark mass,
spotted and bracing itself
for that very moment.

I should be glad. I should
take pride in this burning red slash.
I should finger its texture like

ju-ju beads or memorize the disturbed
skin, the muscles pinched and
prodded and taped back together so

expertly no one would ever know
it had ever gaped open, yawning.
The day will come when,

gazing upon the scar, I will exclaim,
*What a beaut!*
O! the fingers! The fingers

that saved me from some uncertain
future! I should offer them incense, like they do
to the Buddha's sacred knuckle bones.

I should swath them in sweet-smelling
aloes for all they've done. In that
blood-filled moment, they took from me

this dark grace—that which I neither wanted
nor asked for. The knuckles. The haughty
joints, straining so expertly at the latex.

The darkness went, but not
the shame. Those fingers were
unable to slice it at its roots and take

it along. See how it rings my mouth
like milk froth. See how embarrassment
sways in a cold place behind my eyes.

See how well hid the lusts are,
dug in tight behind my aching white
belly button. The year ahead

lies hidden and silent,
there in that gray place I'm headed.
It's neither dusky nor hope-filled

like an Easter morning. It just waits there—
foggy and silent as a fresh-sowed
field. This wound will heal.

The scarred flesh, renewing itself,
will in one perfect moment be made
wonderfully and completely whole.


*February 27*

# This Stigmata

None of them had this stigmata—
not one of those doe-eyed darlings
who cooed their pious love and swayed
into violent ecstasy like beautiful mystical Camilles.

They were content with their bloody shows—
putting even the slaughterhouse sows
to shame, who went complacently to
their triduums even when their bellies
were sliced open and their watery juices gushed out.

This stigmata—
restrained and uncertain—
is so much cleaner. The juices
are clear, the heat of passion
quiet and . . . reserved in a Protestant
sort of way.

And so much closer to those actual pains,
that extreme anxiety that brought on not
the nails and thorns, but sweat—
ugly and like blood, but not blood
or any other sort of gore. It was
instead the passion of stung eyes,
of a face not hidden by a turned-away back,
as Moses strained after, but revealed
in a clear glistening sheen, brighter
than any celestial glow.

This stigmata is not secretive, hidden
behind fingerless gloves or a visored nun's veil.
This stigmata is the divine likeness
revealed and glorified—
unashamedly faced and gloried in.

*February 28*

# Barium

White. Not like milk or sperm, but
like talcum or aspirin. It goes

right down. Dead center. And with
it, the ivory in my mouth grays.

Something hisses. Is it the bitter March morning,
its ice cracking around me? Or is it something else?

I reflect! The stainless steel of the machine
takes me and makes me thin and almost

beautiful again. I'm pulled to
my ends. I'm the size and shape now of

a celery stalk. I'm neon green even. Or
getting there. A dye moves slow

as moss through me—taking its creeping
time working from the needle mark

on my elbow to my lips and back again.
"Inhale," a voice—mechanical and whirring—

instructs. And I do. "Hold it. Hold it."
And I do! I do! I don't flinch even a little as I saw

back and forth inside this whirring zero,
going deep, almost to the hilt. See,

I'm tough. I'm raw as meat. This scar on my belly
is well-earned. My arm—purple as a heart

or an onion—flexes only a bit. My fingers
knead a sweet numbness.

*March 1*

45

# St. David's Day

At the party, one of them—so young
its hurts my face—uncorks
his fizzing coldness and pours
a smoky shot into a glass. Another—
even younger, even more gentle
in her movements—sidles in
beside him, her long white legs
speckled with blue veins. Someone
behind them shouts. Another laughs.
A crackle of applause goes on
like fire in this room.

A beat

                        then a liquor smell fills the air.

Let's sit back
all the way! We've thrown
the sticks! The fortune's read!

Someone here is so sick—
so close to something you—
in this heady innocence
which fogs your eyes like lust—
can only just barely make out
over this music and the steady thump
of your lives. It creaks
in his body. It sounds—
doesn't it?—
like sobbing.

# V

"I lay myself
    in these wounds . . ."

—Georg Christian Lehms

# Tattoos

Not henna but India ink
dots and a needle, like
the tattoos we gave each other

at fourteen. Only no flaming
dragons, no flamboyant hearts
with arrows piercing

them. Only a freckle of blue
here and here and here, like
runway lights to guide the

red pentagram of lasers.
None on the biceps or
the shoulder but on the tender

soft sides where the cold hand
that holds the needle creates
a ripple effect of delight, followed

by a concentrated jab, a piercing
so quick and easy I don't know
how to respond. When it's

done, I wait a moment before
I look. Is it ink? Is it blood?
Or is it water, clear

as a Celtic holy well's,
trickling onto
the white sheet beneath me?

*March 8*

# Desk 42

*"I break out of my body this way,
an annoying miracle."*

—Anne Sexton

Red-faced, I emerge slowly from
the dim-lit room behind Desk 42, where
the TV's blue screen jumped and crackled

and groaned before it turned vibrantly
flesh-colored. Nothing can hide this red that
blooms on my cheeks and neck, not the collar

of my blue shirt, not the cold water I smeared
there with fingers numb and stiff.
And yet, no regrets either. No bridges burned,

no future diverted to a place from which
I cannot retrieve it. This is hope—
pure and gentle and slow as sap.

*Hope* that I placed so carefully
into the blue basket the nurse asked me
to bring to the desk. Nothing

can kill it now—not the streaks of
concentrated X-rays awaiting me
tomorrow, not the carefully manipulated

cold that awaits it—after all those
turbulent, lust-churned years—like a long-
deserved nap. No, not even that can destroy hope.

*March 11*

# Eye

From its place on the ceiling,
the cycloptic red eye winks and
in an instant I am made transparent.
Above and below the fractions of concentrated
light work through me, leaving me

exposed, tender as a cloud.
What more can I do than lie
here, still as furniture?
What more can I do than be
the white canvas for the nurse

to mark her abstract black lines on?
I breathe. I move here or there
as they need me to. I look up, I look
to the side. I am quiet when I need
to be. I laugh when I should. I do

what I'm told to do.
When I finally come down off
the smoky photography glass, I am
stiff and aching. I stumble a little.
Yet I smile and shake my head. And I

wait. What is it my body will do now
to make sense of this invisible intrusion?
It will do the only thing it can—it will leave
a shadow of its self on the table behind me
for them to line me up against tomorrow.

*March 12*

# Thursday in the Fourth Week of Lent

With the hormone balance of a
pregnant woman comes
the nausea, the metallic tastes

haunting the mouth, the repulsion
to food, to lingering scents.
For years I sympathized with the

pregnant. I sorrowed for their pale
faces, their squeezed expressions. The
body changed. It grew, forming

something hard and rotund, then failed.
It was left exhausted and elastic. Then
it began again with a vigor I could not

at the time comprehend. Now more
than empathy. A shared experience—
like stigmata, only bloodless

and with nothing to
culminate into except a
perpetually uncertain recovery.

*March 14*

# Satellite

Whenever I complained about being unlucky—
about being born under some black satellite
that appeared—some dark and
inverted star in the winter sky—

my grandmother agreed. She said,
"yes, it's true" and produced
the evening edition of the Fargo *Forum*
for the day I was born, fingering a side article

mourning the 90 people who
died that morning—breathing their last breath
the exact moment I breathed my first—
when their DC-6 collided into the cold rock

face of a mountain outside Athens.
I spent the better half of my life trying to
counteract the curse some Greek widow
cast on all children born that fateful moment—

trying to outdo whatever evil dogged me from
that first gasp. I tried even to inventory
every hair in my brush, every sliver of fingernail
lest it fall into some gypsy's expert hand.

But it's going now. It's being washed away
like baptism in the swaths of X-rays passing
through my exposed torso each morning. I am
being purified—washed colorless and gentle

as St. Agnes' wool. No crossed fingers. No precious salt
thrown over the shoulder. Rather jolts of
invisible light are burning away the curse. They are
knocking to pieces the gehenna that swam

within me like a rapidly growing mass
no radiologist or X-ray technician could
ever see no matter how hard they looked.
And I emerge from beneath the lens

luckier than the time before. I am lucky! I sing
to the waiting room patients as I pass before
them erect and healthy. I am lucky! As I bound out
the glass doors into the rapidly warming spring morning.

*March 15*

# *Huis Clos*

*"You crazy creature, what do you think
you are doing?"*

—Sartre

So, this is what Sartre wrote about
in *No Exit*—this atheist's hell. They
sit and wait and when their name
is finally called they rise slowly and
go—so trustingly—with the doctors

who float through here
in their clean white coats like stiff,
Protestant angels. These bleached
beings call out names over and over again
over the chatter of people who repeat

to one another, "So we are here forever."
"Forever. My God, how funny! Forever."
If this is hell—or at the very
least some Episcopal purgatory—
then what must heaven be?

Could it be like that
scene in a George C. Scott film
I saw one summer so long ago it
seems to have happened in a dream? In
it, he walks through

some transitory elsewhere of souls,
all of them wearing the scars of
their various deaths—gun-shots and
stitched-back-together decapitations—
as an angelic big band, led by a wingéd

Tommy Dorsey, plays an echoing
"Song of India." Here, there
is no music, only the steady
monotonous thud of a grandfather clock
in one well-lit corner. Here, everyone

knows each other's names, everyone
except me. Mine is the only name not
called out, not pronounced
so carefully, so precisely
there's no doubting who it

might be. The X-ray technician,
glowing white as snow,
knows me and simply seeks out
my pale face amid all these blurring
features. She beckons me with a smile

and a nod and I rise, a little more sure
than the others, grasping my black
coat, and go with her, allowing her
to lead me into those dim caverns of rooms
without a comment or a complaint.

*March 19*

# Two Poems after Neruda

## 1. *Otro*

After wandering around in places
even maps don't show
I finally came to that terrible place

where no one cared
if I ate fat heads of lettuce
slightly brown on the edges

or that incredible mint,
green as elephant dung.
I said nothing—

and in doing so—
kept my heart
yellow as a summer dawn.

## 2. I Went

Only trees, a faint dank
smell of thawing earth and, like that,
a cold spring returns.
With it, the usual vague
hope, elusive and just beyond reach.

The sky dominates with a barely
perceived horizon that goes on
forever until it destroys itself. So!
this is how creation cleanses itself—
this is how it makes itself pure!

I walk into the afternoon, into
gray sky and even grayer snow-covered
earth. But not me—I am not gray.
I am green—like a pine forest
is green. Or my overcoat is
anyway. And with my green self
I carry a headiness that
sways within me like a
fever, while a heaviness clutches at
my aching ankles with
every step I take.

Snow! O snow! Come!
Come to me in this place
of such anguished stillness!

*March 22*

# Yellow

*tengo el corazón amarillo*

—Pablo Neruda

Neruda's sick-world was
yellow. Something ebbed
slower and slower within
him in those last days,
their mornings, noons
and dusks tinged with
yellow. It was amber—
so very much unlike
any I can even
imagine. It was molten and
all-encompassing like
a pumice that held him
stock still in its hue.

His dying heart was
filled with yellow
and so too were his poems—
the images, smelling
sweeter than that gorgeous
Pacific he wrapped
his words within.

Yellow flooded his eyes—
those same eyes that
within the year
would film over, turn gray
and would fold back
into their dark holds. In the end
there was nothing but yellow,

the vibrant colors—
the lush greens, the deep
oceanic blues—
baked to this most final
lasting tint.

My world—colorless and
snow-filled—is so much less
dramatic. Mine is a place
where silver balloons
wilt and glide—
lower and slower—
for the floor—
where even the flowers
my friends sent me
lost their colors as quickly
as I touched them—shedding
their reds and blues
and purples like pollen. See how
the colors lie there like
shadows at the base of
the vase. Like his last color,
what is left is
perfectly colorless—perfectly
perfect in that effortless
sort of way.

*March 22*

# Echo

"*Who*
*says that everything died for us*
*when our eyes broke?*
*Everything awakened, everything began.*"
—Paul Celan

I'm pure! See how pure I am!
I must be. Only the pure can be
denied such basic recognitions—
your last name, its hard consonants
pronounced so perfectly, the gabled house
you longed for, that cool green plot

beside you in the cemetery
which now lies there awaiting
someone else's sweet sleep.
I *am* pure—pure as anything
severed at its root.
Only the pure

can smolder here,
incised and gruff, puffed
up with a sweet lingering
radiation. Turn off the lights—
let's see if I glow. Let' see
if I'll flicker and flutter

in the dark like a green
night light.
The gritty muck has
been polished away.
What is left is pristine.
I am brilliant!

Can't you see that? I have
become so sweetly vestal.
Look how I blush
when I touch your pillow,
my face flushed red with sin.
Look how my fingers

come away thick and musty with
your sex-smell. No, don't worry.
Not even that can defile me.
I go about now leaving
not even a trace of myself
behind me. I'm disappearing,

folding back into the shadows
as simply as the night
swallows its moon-tinted
clouds. Take notice
while you can. What
these last shimmers do —

dancing on my still
amazed face. See how
I sway and shimmy
on your cheek like a blush.
Before you know it
I'll be gone.

Nothing dramatic. Just a very
slight sigh, left hanging
near the ceiling of some
barely-lit room. Other than
that, there will only be
a spring thaw.

A staring watch.
Displaced sod.
A steady humming
coming from
somewhere not
all that far away.

*March 25*

# Ash—the Loam

It *will* happen—whether creeping
up, lethal and ugly, through my body or
in some merciful instant I can neither plan for

nor even, at this moment, imagine. When it does,
do this for me if you will—bury my ashes here
in the cool shadow of the black granite stone

my father and I set into place just
a few autumns ago. Bury them here—
where the black loam, broken

by the neighbor's pole digger, will
yawn open for the urn and take it
into its silent embrace. I can't imagine

anything better for myself—
not the fine-ground bones
released into some unrelenting

gust, nor sealed up in a sterile
marble vault in the cathedral. *This* will
do. *This* appeals to me. When I

think beyond that last exhausted breath
I can easily imagine
whatever's left still here, even

in that inconceivable future, set here
by those I loved and will probably
still love in some way I can only

just barely comprehend now. *The Book
of Common Prayer* committal, its precise,
centuries-old formula, will please me

if I am able to be pleased and able too
to observe it from some place near
and yet not so near. How often I stood

on the lip of someone else's grave
and thought of my own far-off (or so
I thought) burial. It is not fear or apprehension

I feel when I think of it but
completeness. Ash—the loam—
the prayers so familiar I could

pray them for myself before sleep—
yes, this is what I want. Bury my ashes
and leave them in this place I have come to

love with an affection only one
who loves the earth in just this wonderfully
perfect way can ever fully understand.


*March 26*


65

# Embracing the Floor

*"Music, Italian music in Dakota."*
—Whitman

*Castrati* sing—pure as a
spring thaw—from the stereo,
something baroque and
blessedly Italian as I, solemn
as a desert abba, fast

and pray and bow, surrounded
by ikons and softly glowing
candles. I don't even know
who I am anymore. Who is
this person whose voice I expected

to change, to go an octave higher?
Who is this monk who, like
the prophet-eunuch Daniel,
squares his shoulders and falls
so easily—

so humbly and without
a whimper—
into the deep pit?
Where did the limp go?
Where has the aching

hip hid itself? Why is
the walk so much
smoother?  Watch me!
Just watch! I'm perfecting
myself. Watch how

I lose my balance,
how I—
my body cruciform—
embrace the floor
with ease!


*March 31*

# Easter

We wake early into
this blue dawn—

into this weirdest of
light the moon still gives

at this hour. We ready
ourselves in only that

way we can—
the water still cold

on our pale cheeks,
our shirts stiff, our pants

creased and pleated.
It is Easter. The birds peal

the dawn that happens—
unseen by us—

behind the horizon and
the heavy layer of morning

clouds that gather there.
Mists of escaping frost

haunt the churchyard—
fumey gray selves moving

among the leaning stones,
obliterating the moss-encrusted

epitaphs and the close-
cropped brown lawn.

Our ashes will one day lie there,
beneath the polished black stone

we can just barely make out
at this early hour. The earth

breathes. It does! We hear
it. There is a steady

sighing coming up through
the ground as we walk

across the parking lot into
the hushed enclosure of the church.

When the sun finally breaks through
the clouds, it spills into

the nave distorted. Prisms of
blue and purple fall over

the wooden sills and onto
our laps in slashing haphazard

streaks. Somehow it softens
the stiffness of holiness that

lingers about somewhere
above our heads. It highlights

the white faith of resurrection—
hueing it with an underlying

yellow. We know
without saying it or professing it;

*this* is what Easter is—
a careful faith that persisted

through winter, precise liturgy,
pronounced with well-placed

inflection. And a hope
so sacred it almost embarrasses us.

*March 31*

# Horizon

*after the last treatment*

From what star-filled
place did you come? From

what snowy destination
across that river did you

appear, swirling with
snow? Out of the west

you came—like a cloud,
only swifter and more

sure of yourself. Out of
the west you came

and rescued me.
You saw the tire—

destroyed by a rock
left recklessly on the blacktop

by a plow. You
saw how it shriveled

and filled the air with
the skunk-like stench of

burned rubber. You saw
me, standing there

alongside the highway,
five miles from town, late

spring snowflakes
fluttering above me as

though they were waiting . . .
waiting for me to lie

down there exhausted
beneath them.

Did you know I couldn't
flag anyone down?

I couldn't step out
from behind the pickup,

embarrassed by my paleness, by
the threat of vomiting and

diarrhea, by standing there
helpless, along the cold gray

concrete . . . so helpless, I
almost returned to the cab

instead of waiting. Waiting . . .
For what? For some comet to

streak through the endless
gray sky, its tail somehow

more icy than this bitter wind,
giving me a sign of hope? or for

an angel . . .
an uninvoked being sent

to me in that desolation—
not only of the place I was trapped

within, but of my unforgiving
and betrayed body.

It was then you saw me
as I stood there, the semis

flying past me, rattling chains,
leaving thin wisps of snow

dancing behind them on
the pavement. Did you

hear my sighs? Did you
listen when I wondered

to myself, if I had ever
been this sick? If I had

ever been so weak I couldn't
change even a tire?

It was then you stopped and
gave me a lift to that place you

were headed toward. It was then
you grasped me and insisted

I come. "Come!" you said
and I was too weak, too

overwhelmed with gratitude
not to go. Or was it

something more
that compelled me? Was it

the unspoken cancer in
you drawing with some

cosmic magnetism at
the empty place within me

where another cancer lurked? Or was it
simply two people on

the edge of some vast white
expanse, barely meeting, barely

exchanging more than a few
dozen words, and never

any more, and one of those words,
"cancer," tossed back and forth

between us, recklessly? Was that all?
And like the wingéd stranger

who snatched up Ezekiel
by his hair and

set him down in that
dry cold land of bones, so you

let me down on the
cold sidewalk

before the tire store and,
with only a wave and a smiling

nod, were whisked away
into the whirling snow. Nothing

more. No names, no promise
to see each other again, for how

could we? Just me standing
there unable to say a thing

and you, ascending
nameless and without

a flaw in my memory
of you, into a rapidly

dusk-filled horizon
of snow.

*April 8*

# Almost Pentecost

It's almost
overwhelming how

the lilacs'
scents

haunt every nook
and cranny. Every

which way I turn,
my nose shudders

with the onslaught
of their smell. Pentecost

is a whole week
away. By then,

they will
have darkened, their

petals shed
to reveal the dark

skeleton of the bush.
The dusk

will hide more
than I can imagine

in the shadows that
lengthen across

the yard. Now,
it's the lilacs and

the smells of lilacs
in every room. I close

my eyes and
it's lilacs I see

hanging above me,
airy but not purple.

They're white—
the color of the noonday sky—

white as the tongues of
light that await

their awesome
descent

a week from now.
Only there will

be no gift of
interpretation.

The acts of this
spring will never—

*should* never—
be recounted

and celebrated with
streamers bright

as a Communist
Youth Rally

held high in procession
through the dark nave.

No rushing wind
will swipe through

and cleanse the muck
left by the tardy thaw

of this awful spring.
I open my eyes and see

a perfect reflection,
shimmering

against the high plaster.
See how the ceiling

somehow welcomes
the light, darkening

only slightly to
the pink color of

flesh as today's dusk
begins to reveal itself.


*May 11*

# VI

*O benediction!*

*"All shall be well, and all shall be well; all manner of things shall be well."*

—Julian of Norwich

# Bed Sheet

*after the 6 month's checkup*

We forget it, the way
we forget the floods or
those unpleasant neighbors

who shrivel and die away
only to have us attend their
funerals with not an emotion

or a false condolence. The word
is easy to say now since it happened
and was taken care of. We can say it—

and I do—because it is no longer
dangerous, no longer an
invocation.  It won't happen

again, the doctor said, and it won't. It
won't! because I never heard him
say that one word

"probably."
I did hear him when he said
I have fifty more years—"at least"—

that insurmountable number.
Fifty years. Fifty years more and
look at me. I can already barely

remember the feel of it, the
discomfort I felt in January when
I went around, knees in, as though I

were protecting it. Fifty more years
and . . . oh, who knows? See how we
forget it, how it goes, fleeing in our

memories? See how we
talk of it as though it
happened to those ornery

neighbors whose graves
lie sagging and forgotten
just down the road,

covered in dandelions
and a caked top layer
of sod. It happened

and now it doesn't
and, before me lie
fifty years laid out, blank

as a just-ironed bed sheet.
It's so clean and crisp
I almost can't step forward

and rumple even
the corner
closest to me.


*August 22*

# Chaos Without

We fear airplanes now and
the sound of them too. We
fear their rippling shadows
and wonder if their lights blinking
at us ominously is a Morse
Code. We fear our knowledge
of what a cylinder of metal
and two slicing wings can do—
how in a blink of an eye—
that's all it takes, we know now—
they can unfold blooms of
flames and smoke like some
lethal party trick.

They're easy to fear. We're
reminded of them almost
daily. We see them gliding
low, jagged landing gear reaching out
at us from below, as they
come in for landings and
nosing into the sky at take-off.
It's easy to fear what
we can identify. Not at all
like the blooming that happens
within—secretly, painlessly,
like a gathering of conspirators.

That morning, when I awoke,
I was off. I felt something
nagging at me like a cold
I couldn't shake. Was it there
even then, dividing and dividing,
devising some grand appearance

five months later? Was it only
beginning in those moments
before the news broke and the slow
realization of chaos descended
with agonizing trepidation.? Chaos
and chaos to follow. Chaos without
and chaos within.

We fear airplanes now, yes.
But I fear that and more. My breath
catches with any slight disturbance—
any suspicious shadow
on the horizon or on my still-pale
flesh. I fear coughs that
last too long or aches that linger.
I fret when I lose a pound
or gain two. I am as careful when
looking in the mirror as
at the skies. Chaos without and
chaos within—even now
one year later and knowing
all we know.

*September 11*

# Dusk

We rise with the road
into a dusk that happens
more suddenly
than we're used to—

caused by the undulation
of hills hardened by a frost
that took hold
weeks early and will stay

now for good. When we
follow the crest, we find below us
a spread-out carpet of lights
from one rapidly darkening

horizon to another.
I am silent as we descend, the
way lit by a pair of dull
headlights, made duller by

the fact that a shadow of the
day behind us still
lingers in the sky despite
the overcast. In the dark hills

deer move carefully. We see their
shifting forms and the unblinking
neon of their eyes when a headlight
glides over them.

Shards of broken
ice lie along the pavement and
suddenly I remember the ice
last spring and how stubborn

it was, refusing to give up
even a trickle of itself
to the rapidly warming light.
Now the light, so much less

stubborn, fails and as it does,
the ice forms, persistent as
the dusk that envelops us
so quickly.

As we glide into this isolated
northern city, I am suddenly
overjoyed for no real reason.
One moment, I feel little

or nothing. The next, something
pure and gorgeous wells up within me—
so uncontrollable I gasp out loud.
It is just then I realize, for the first time

in months, that I am *well*—
truly and wonderfully well.
And when I think I can't
stand the gurgling emotion

that overflows my lips and escapes
me, I look up into the sky
and see it—a transformation
so subtle I almost didn't notice it

as I sit there trembling
beyond the tinted windshield.
I say to myself
"Look! Just look!!

"Look how the dusk—
full of clouds and gloom—
has dissolved into
multitudes of stars!"                    *November 1*

# Nine Months

*in memory*
*Emma Ness*

Nine months and this is where
I am. The plastic square
high on the columbarium wall
hides what did not go down into

the earth. The stone plate that
will cover it won't be set into
place for another week, your
name inscribed on it and stenciled

black—just your name and dates
and nothing more. Beneath the
covering bits of bone, some thin
as fingernail clippings, others jagged

and ghastly, lie quietly in their
black polypropylene urn. A
spray of cornflowers
wilts, discarded, behind the altar,

their black-edged blooms curling
inward. A faded pink ribbon
sheds glitter across the stone floor
you walked upon countless times.

I stomp the floor, feel
it resist the toe of my
shoe, feel it resound, giving
way to nothing. Only a

squelched sighing comes
from somewhere high
above me, near the wooden
buttresses on the chapel ceiling.

There is no wind. No sound
of any sort except the slightly
desperate echo of my own
breathing. Yet I wonder . . . if I

put my ear to the wall, could I hear
it—a pulse maybe, one lingering
gasp of life, leaving
its sad impression in the marble lining

like a fossil. Though the cremation
was thorough, something
continues. The heat the flames
kindled has not given way

entirely to a dry permanence
and silence. No. Something
remains, hunkered down within
the stone abscess. How is it, I ask

whatever warm after-embryo lies
burrowed above my head. How is it
that you ended up here and I . . .
I stand beneath you, my fingers

numb, my cheeks pale
with exhaustion. How is it that I
had it easy—the easiest of
remissions, while you . . .

you burned in those last
days. A fire roared in you,
behind the ribs. You shuddered.
You gasped. You clenched

my knuckles once, twice.
And then! it was done.
What killed you lingered. You
smoldered with it for months.

You refused to name it,
to call it anything, as though it
were nothing more than the
beginning embers of some

simmering summer fever. You only
said, "there's a buzz—a buzz, a
buzz buzzing, humming in
my ear wherever I go. A filth dogs

me like . . . sin. O sin! We know it,
don't we, you and I? Gnawing at
us day and night like this." Sunlight
falls through the highest

oval window, stained blue
and pink and yellow. It
sticks in my hair like a
sticky coiffure. It falls as well
on the gilt cross above the altar.

It casts beneath it a triangulated
shadow—perfectly and
appropriately trinitarian. The light
shifts and a smattering of bright

multi-colored speckles
dot not only the wall,
but the exposed niche. And
with it there . . .

silence. Face it, I tell myself. Nothing lingers here, except a persistent mourning. Sound has long since been aborted. Its umbulicus is severed.

*November 20*

# Mercy

*"He thought of what was in store for him. Whatever it might be, he knew that all would be well."*
—Aldous Huxley

The old self—the one
who brought the new year in

angry and bitter—has died. He
went quietly, unabsolved

and damned to an afterlife
of perpetual disgust.

I have emerged from his
ashes with my hair cut

short as a zen monk's.
Like a monk, I have sworn off meat—

the greasy pork, the ground-
up beef bloody with death,

the cold gray-tummied fish. Even
my voice changed—the stiff accent

lost to a voice ten years older
and slightly Northeastern. The recorded

message on the phone is
now useless and juvenile.

I don't even look the same. The people
who knew me better than anyone else didn't even

recognize me when I arose, white-
albed, from the thick fog that held me.

Even the love they felt for me was different—
so much more intense, so strange and

awkward like a stale room.
I shed my old self—throwing it

out like dirty font water—and
walked into this strange new self, who

clicks his tongue and sings—
listen to him

as he *sings!*—
*O benediction! O buona ventura!*


*December 31*

Jamie Parsley is a poet and an Episcopal priest. Born and raised near Fargo, North Dakota, he is the author of six books of poems: *Paper Doves, Falling and Other Poems* (1992); *The Loneliness of Blizzards* (1995); *Cloud: A Poem in 2 Acts* (1997); *The Wounded Table* (1999); *no stars, no moon* (2004) and *Ikon* (2005). His poems and fiction have been published in a variety of literary journals in the United States, Britain, Japan and Canada. He received his MFA from Vermont College and currently serves as Assistant to the Bishop for Communications for the Episcopal Diocese of North Dakota and teaches at the University of Mary, Fargo. In 2004 he was designated an Associate Poet Laureate of North Dakota.